EASY BROADWAY
Duets

7 GREAT ARRANGEMENTS
BY GLENDA AUSTIN, ERIC BAUMGARTNER AND CAROLYN MILLER

INCLUDES ONLINE AUDIO

The online audio tracks give you the flexibility to rehearse or perform these piano duets anytime and anywhere. Each piece features a Secondo part, a Primo part, and a demo track of both parts together that can be downloaded or streamed. The *Playback+* feature allows you to change the tempo without altering the pitch!

PLAYBACK+
Speed • Pitch • Balance • Loop

To access audio visit:
www.halleonard.com/mylibrary
Enter Code
4218-1365-0616-7213

ISBN 978-1-4950-2128-2

WILLIS MUSIC

EXCLUSIVELY DISTRIBUTED BY

HAL•LEONARD®
CORPORATION
7777 W. BLUEMOUND RD. P.O. BOX 13819 MILWAUKEE, WI 53213

Visit Hal Leonard Online at
www.halleonard.com

CONTENTS

4

Close Every Door
from JOSEPH AND THE AMAZING TECHNICOLOR® DREAMCOAT

SECONDO

Music by Andrew Lloyd Webber
Lyrics by Tim Rice
Arranged by Glenda Austin

Tranquil

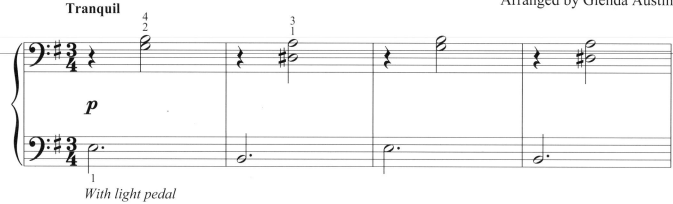

With light pedal

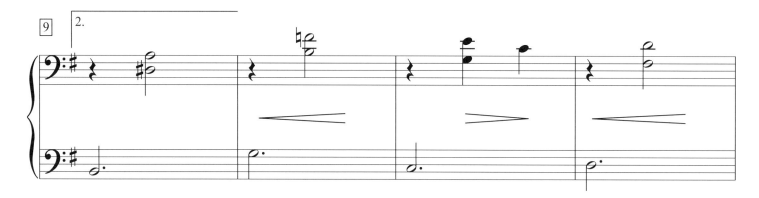

Close Every Door
from JOSEPH AND THE AMAZING TECHNICOLOR® DREAMCOAT

PRIMO

Music by Andrew Lloyd Webber
Lyrics by Tim Rice
Arranged by Glenda Austin

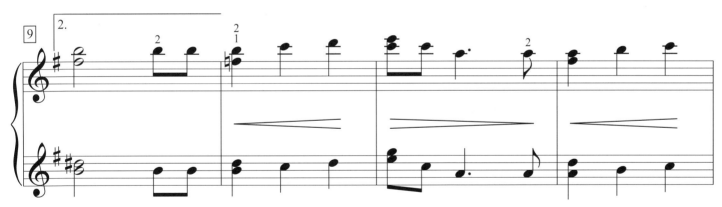

6

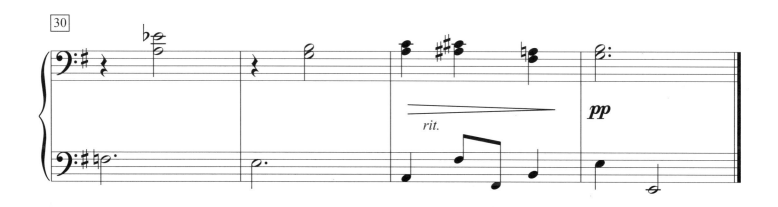

PRIMO

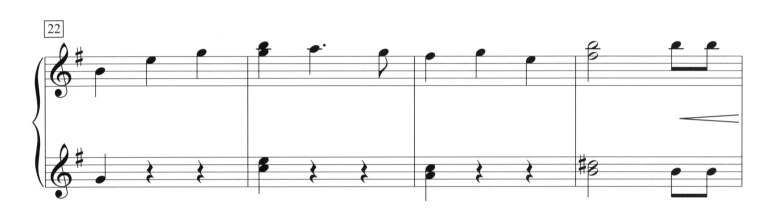

Happiness

from YOU'RE A GOOD MAN, CHARLIE BROWN

SECONDO

Words and Music by Clark Gesner
Arranged by Glenda Austin

Cheerfully, with a bounce

Happiness

from YOU'RE A GOOD MAN, CHARLIE BROWN

PRIMO

Words and Music by Clark Gesner
Arranged by Glenda Austin

Cheerfully, with a bounce

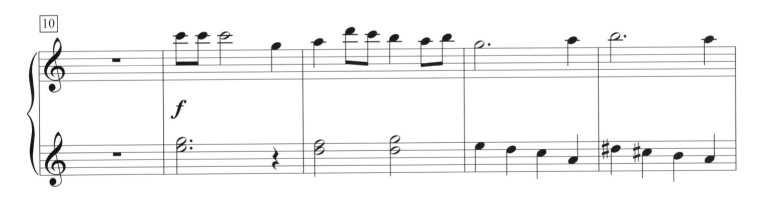

SECONDO

PRIMO

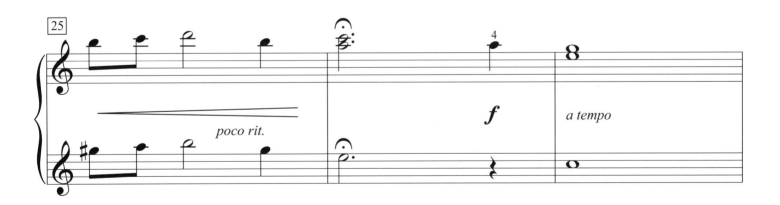

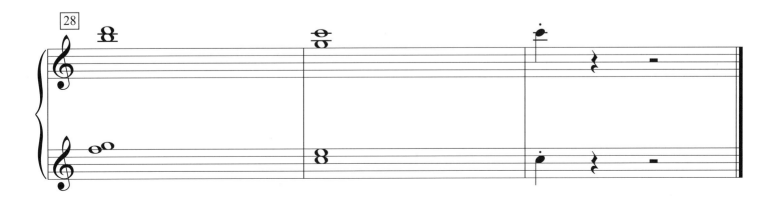

I Whistle a Happy Tune

from THE KING AND I

SECONDO

Lyrics by Oscar Hammerstein II
Music by Richard Rodgers
Arranged by Glenda Austin

Moderato, blissfully

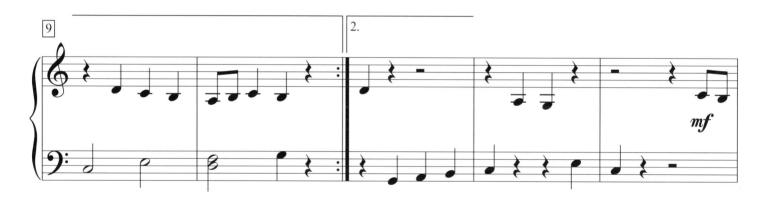

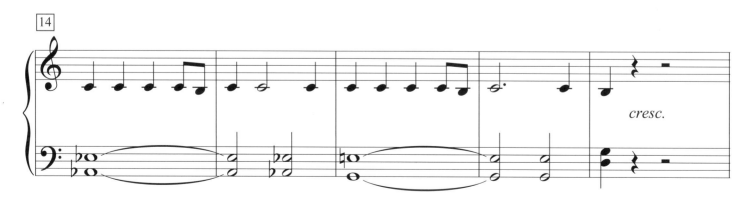

I Whistle a Happy Tune

from THE KING AND I

PRIMO

Lyrics by Oscar Hammerstein II
Music by Richard Rodgers
Arranged by Glenda Austin

Moderato, blissfully

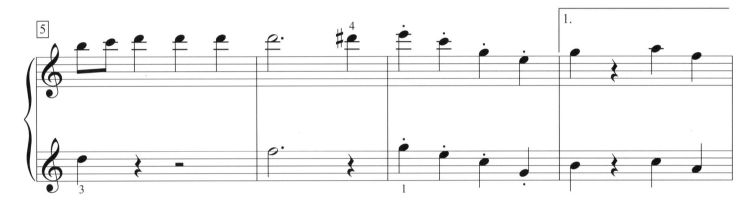

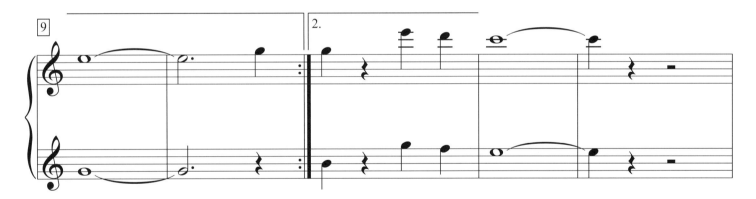

SECONDO

PRIMO

Matchmaker
from the Musical FIDDLER ON THE ROOF

SECONDO

Words by Sheldon Harnick
Music by Jerry Bock
Arranged by Eric Baumgartner

Matchmaker
from the Musical FIDDLER ON THE ROOF

PRIMO

Words by Sheldon Harnick
Music by Jerry Bock
Arranged by Eric Baumgartner

Bright waltz tempo

R.H. measures 1-15 tacet first time

mf

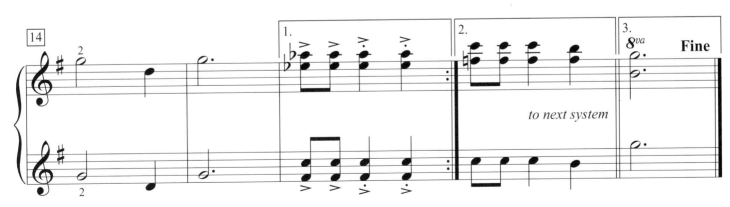

to next system

Fine

SECONDO

D.C. al Fine
(3rd ending)

PRIMO

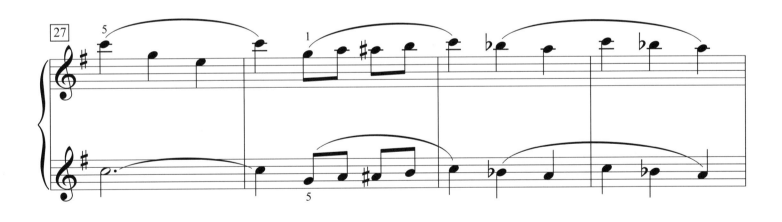

**D.C. al Fine
(3rd ending)**

On My Own

from LES MISÉRABLES

SECONDO

Music by Claude-Michel Schönberg
Lyrics by Alain Boublil, Jean-Marc Natel,
Herbert Kretzmer, John Caird and Trevor Nunn
Arranged by Carolyn Miller

On My Own

from LES MISÉRABLES

PRIMO

Music by Claude-Michel Schönberg
Lyrics by Alain Boublil, Jean-Marc Natel,
Herbert Kretzmer, John Caird and Trevor Nunn
Arranged by Carolyn Miller

SECONDO

PRIMO

The Phantom of the Opera

from THE PHANTOM OF THE OPERA

SECONDO

Music by Andrew Lloyd Webber
Lyrics by Charles Hart
Additional Lyrics by Richard Stilgoe and Mike Batt
Arranged by Eric Baumgartner

The Phantom of the Opera
from THE PHANTOM OF THE OPERA

PRIMO

Music by Andrew Lloyd Webber
Lyrics by Charles Hart
Additional Lyrics by Richard Stilgoe and Mike Batt
Arranged by Eric Baumgartner

SECONDO

PRIMO

The Sound of Music
from THE SOUND OF MUSIC

SECONDO

Lyrics by Oscar Hammerstein II
Music by Richard Rodgers
Arranged by Carolyn Miller

The Sound of Music

from THE SOUND OF MUSIC

PRIMO

Lyrics by Oscar Hammerstein II
Music by Richard Rodgers
Arranged by Carolyn Miller

SECONDO

PRIMO

Glenda Austin is a composer, arranger, pianist, and teacher from Joplin, Missouri. A graduate of the University of Missouri, Glenda teaches music in elementary and high school, and is an adjunct faculty member at Missouri Southern State University. She is a frequent adjudicator and clinician for Willis and Hal Leonard, presenting piano workshops for teachers and students throughout the United States, as well as in Canada and Japan. Several of Glenda's compositions appear on state repertoire lists, and two best-sellers, "Jazz Suite No. 2" and "Sea Nocturne," are perennial favorites on the National Federation list.

Eric Baumgartner received jazz degrees from Berklee College of Music in Boston and DePaul University in Chicago. He is the author and creator of the *Jazzabilities* and *Jazz Connection* series, a related set of beginning jazz piano books. Besides composing and maintaining a teaching studio, Eric works extensively in musical theatre and plays keyboard and guitar with several pop and jazz groups. He is the orchestrator of several noted Willis publications, including the *Teaching Little Fingers to Play* series, *Popular Piano Solos,* and his own *Jazz It Up!* series. His wide range of musical influences is reflected in his balanced approach to teaching: he finds validity in all music and works with students to help them find their own musical identity through improvising, arranging, and composing. Eric has presented his unique teaching techniques in the United States, England, and Australia.

Carolyn Miller holds a bachelor's degree from the College Conservatory of Music at the University of Cincinnati and a master's degree in elementary education from Xavier University. A lifelong educator, Carolyn has taught piano to students of all ages, privately and in the classroom, and continues to maintain a piano studio in her Cincinnati home. She presents workshops throughout the United States and is often asked to adjudicate at music festivals and competitions. Carolyn's music often teaches essential technical skills, yet is fun to play, making it appealing to children and adults and resulting in frequent appearances on the National Federation list. In fact, well-known personality Regis Philbin performed two of her compositions, "Rolling River" and "Fireflies," live on national television.